# The Battle Between Apple The Big Tech And Government

## Navigating Legal Storms In The Tech Industry And Exploring The Battle Between Innovation And Regulation In Silicon Valley.

Julia J. Scott

Copyright © 2024  Julia J. Scott

All rights reserved. No part of this publication may be reproduced, distributed, or transmitted in any form or by any means, including photocopying, recording, or other electronic or mechanical methods, without the prior written permission of the publisher, except in the case of brief quotations embodied in critical reviews and certain other noncommercial uses permitted by copyright law.

# Table Of Contents

Introduction

Chapter One; The U.S. Department of Justice vs. Apple

Chapter Two; Allegations Against Apple

Chapter Three; Apple's Response and Denial

Chapter Four; The Broader Antitrust Crackdown on Big Tech

Chapter Five; Impact on the Tech Industry

Chapter Six; President Biden's Antitrust Agenda

Chapter Seven; Legal Landscape and Precedents

Chapter Eight; Consumer Perspectives

**Chapter Nine; The Chamber of Progress's Critique**

**Chapter Ten; International Ramifications**

# Introduction

In a world where technology reigns supreme, the giants of the tech industry wield immense power and influence, shaping the way we communicate, work, and live our lives. Among these titans stands Apple Inc., a company synonymous with innovation, creativity, and cutting-edge technology.

But behind the sleek designs and revolutionary products lies a complex web of legal battles, regulatory scrutiny, and ethical dilemmas that have captured the attention of the world. Welcome to the gripping tale of "Apple Under Fire: Navigating the Antitrust Storm."

In this book, we embark on a journey into the heart of one of the most iconic companies of our time, exploring the controversies, challenges, and triumphs that have defined Apple's tumultuous relationship with antitrust regulators and the broader tech industry.

From the halls of justice to the boardrooms of Silicon Valley, we uncover the high-stakes battles that have unfolded between Apple and government authorities, as well as the broader implications for competition, innovation, and consumer welfare.

Through a meticulous examination of legal filings, industry reports, and expert analysis, we seek to unravel the complexities of antitrust law and its impact on one of the world's most valuable companies.

But this book is not just about legal proceedings and regulatory crackdowns; it's also a story of innovation, ambition, and the relentless pursuit of excellence. We delve into the history of Apple, tracing its humble beginnings in a garage to its meteoric rise as a global technology powerhouse.

Along the way, we meet the visionaries, innovators, and disruptors who have shaped Apple's journey, from Steve Jobs and Steve Wozniak to Tim Cook and beyond. As we navigate the twists and turns of Apple's antitrust saga, we confront challenging questions about the nature of competition, the role of government intervention, and the future of the tech industry.

Through thought-provoking analysis and engaging storytelling, we aim to shed light on the complexities of modern capitalism and the ongoing struggle to balance innovation with accountability. So join us as we embark on this captivating odyssey through the corridors of power, the halls of justice, and the cutting-edge labs where tomorrow's technologies are born.

Whether you're a tech enthusiast, a legal scholar, or simply a curious observer, "Apple Under Fire" promises to captivate, educate, and inspire as we uncover the untold story behind one of the world's most iconic companies. Get ready to dive deep into the heart of the antitrust storm and discover the secrets of Apple's enduring legacy in the digital age.

# Chapter One; The U.S. Department Of Justice vs. Apple

The legal showdown between the U.S. Department of Justice and Apple has captured the attention of the tech world and beyond. This high-stakes battle pits one of the largest tech companies in the world against the might of the U.S. government.

At the heart of the dispute lies accusations of monopolistic practices within the smartphone market, with Apple accused of wielding its dominance to stifle competition and harm consumers. The Department of Justice, alongside attorneys general from 15 states and the District of Columbia, has launched a landmark lawsuit against Apple, alleging a range of antitrust violations.

These allegations include claims that Apple restricts its smartphone operating system in ways that drive up costs for consumers and limit the ability of developers to release products on rival platforms.

In a bold move, the Department of Justice has taken aim at some of Apple's core practices. One of the central allegations is that Apple obstructs the development of what the DOJ terms "super apps," which would enable users to seamlessly switch between different smartphone platforms.

Additionally, the lawsuit contends that Apple prevents the creation of cloud-streaming apps that could offer high-quality gaming experiences without the need for additional hardware.

Furthermore, Apple is accused of hindering the development of cross-platform messaging apps, effectively locking users into its ecosystem and preventing them from switching to rival devices. The lawsuit marks a significant escalation in the ongoing battle between Big Tech and government regulators.

Attorney General Merrick Garland emphasized the importance of holding companies accountable for antitrust violations, stating that consumers should not be forced to pay higher prices due to companies flouting antitrust laws.

Apple's dominance in the market has not gone unnoticed, with its market capitalization surpassing the GDP of numerous countries. However, the Department of Justice contends that Apple's success is not solely due to superior products but also through exclusionary tactics that harm competition.

Apple has vehemently denied the allegations leveled against it, dismissing the lawsuit as government overreach. The company argues that it is under no obligation to adopt designs or policies preferred by competitors if they would compromise the user experience.

For example, Apple cites its decision not to develop a version of iMessage compatible with non-iPhone devices, asserting that such a move would fail to meet its standards for user experience. Apple's statement emphasizes its commitment to innovation and creating products that resonate with consumers, while also warning of the potential consequences of government intervention in technology design.

The lawsuit against Apple forms part of President Joe Biden's broader antitrust crackdown on Big Tech. With ongoing antitrust cases against other tech giants like Google, Meta (formerly Facebook), and Amazon, the Biden administration is signaling its determination to rein in the power of dominant tech companies.

The case against Apple represents the third attempt by an attorney general to challenge the company, marking the most comprehensive effort to date. The allegations against Apple extend beyond the smartphone market, encompassing a wide range of services and industries.

From web browsers to entertainment and automotive services, the lawsuit paints a picture of Apple's monopoly stretching across various sectors. The Department of Justice accuses Apple of employing a range of restrictive contractual rules and restrictions to stifle competition and extract higher prices from consumers.

Assistant Attorney General Jonathan Kanter asserts that the lawsuit seeks to hold Apple accountable and prevent it from deploying similar tactics in other vital markets. Not everyone is in agreement with the Department of Justice's stance. The Chamber of Progress, a trade group representing tech companies like Apple, has criticized the lawsuit, arguing that consumers value the highly curated mobile ecosystem offered by Apple.

Chamber of Progress CEO Adam Kovacevich contends that forcing Apple to open up its software and hardware would deprive consumers of choice and homogenize the smartphone market.

Apple's legal woes are not confined to the United States. Earlier this month, the European Union imposed a hefty fine of $2 billion on Apple for restricting competition in the music-streaming services sector. Apple has announced its intention to appeal the decision, signaling its determination to fight back against regulatory scrutiny on both sides of the Atlantic.

As the legal battle unfolds, the outcome will have far-reaching implications for the future of competition in the tech industry. Whether Apple will emerge victorious or face significant regulatory constraints remains to be seen. However, one thing is certain: the clash between Big Tech and government regulators is far from over, and the outcome will shape the landscape of the digital economy for years to come.

# Chapter Two; Allegations Against Apple

Accusations leveled against tech giant Apple have thrust the company into the spotlight, igniting a fierce legal battle with far-reaching implications. The allegations, brought forth by the U.S. Department of Justice and joined by attorneys general from 15 states and the District of Columbia, paint a damning picture of Apple's conduct in the smartphone market.

At the crux of the dispute lies the accusation of monopolistic practices, with Apple accused of wielding its market dominance to stifle competition and harm consumers. The lawsuit alleges a range of antitrust violations, with the Department of Justice asserting that Apple's actions restrict competition and drive up costs for consumers.

Among the key allegations is Apple's purported obstruction of what the DOJ terms "super apps" — applications that would enable users to seamlessly transition between different smartphone platforms. Additionally, Apple is accused of impeding the development of cloud-streaming apps, which would allow for high-quality gaming experiences without the need for additional hardware.

Moreover, the lawsuit contends that Apple actively inhibits the creation of cross-platform messaging apps, effectively locking users into its ecosystem and limiting choice in the marketplace. The legal battle between Apple and the Department of Justice represents a significant escalation in the ongoing scrutiny of Big Tech by government regulators.

Attorney General Merrick Garland underscored the importance of holding companies accountable for antitrust violations, emphasizing that consumers should not bear the brunt of inflated prices resulting from anticompetitive behavior.

Despite Apple's considerable success in the market — with a market capitalization surpassing the GDP of numerous countries — the Department of Justice maintains that such success is not solely attributable to superior products but also to exclusionary tactics employed by the company.

Apple has vehemently denied the allegations, dismissing the lawsuit as government overreach. The company contends that it is not obligated to adopt designs or policies preferred by competitors if doing so would compromise the user experience.

For example, Apple points to its decision not to develop a version of iMessage compatible with non-iPhone devices, citing concerns about maintaining its standards for user experience. Apple's statement emphasizes its commitment to innovation and creating products that resonate with consumers, while also warning of the potential consequences of government intervention in technology design.

The lawsuit against Apple forms part of a broader antitrust crackdown on Big Tech by the Biden administration. With ongoing antitrust cases against other tech giants like Google, Meta (formerly Facebook), and Amazon, the government is signaling its determination to rein in the power of dominant tech companies.

The case against Apple marks the third attempt by an attorney general to challenge the company, representing the most comprehensive effort to date to address alleged anticompetitive practices in the smartphone market. The allegations against Apple extend beyond the realm of smartphones, encompassing various services and industries.

From web browsers to entertainment and automotive services, the lawsuit alleges that Apple's monopoly spans across multiple sectors. Assistant Attorney General Jonathan Kanter asserts that the lawsuit seeks to hold Apple accountable and prevent it from deploying similar tactics in other vital markets.

Not all parties agree with the Department of Justice's stance. The Chamber of Progress, a trade group representing tech companies like Apple, has criticized the lawsuit, arguing that consumers value the highly curated mobile ecosystem offered by Apple.

Chamber of Progress CEO Adam Kovacevich contends that forcing Apple to open up its software and hardware would deprive consumers of choice and homogenize the smartphone market. Apple's legal woes are not limited to the United States.

Earlier this month, the European Union imposed a hefty fine of $2 billion on Apple for restricting competition in the music-streaming services sector. Apple has announced its intention to appeal the decision, signaling its determination to fight back against regulatory scrutiny on both sides of the Atlantic.

As the legal battle unfolds, the outcome will have profound implications for the future of competition in the tech industry. Whether Apple emerges victorious or faces significant regulatory constraints remains to be seen. However, one thing is clear: the clash between Big Tech and government regulators is far from over, and the resolution of this dispute will shape the landscape of the digital economy for years to come.

# Chapter Three; Apple's Response And Denial

Apple's stance in response to the allegations leveled against it by the U.S. Department of Justice and a coalition of state attorneys general has been resolute and unyielding. In a bold assertion of its innocence, Apple has vehemently denied the accusations of anticompetitive behavior, portraying the lawsuit as an unjustified attack on its business practices.

The company's response, while expectedly defensive, offers insights into its perspective on the unfolding legal saga and sheds light on its strategic approach to navigating the complex terrain of antitrust regulation. At the heart of Apple's defense is the assertion that it has not violated antitrust laws and that its actions are justified by its commitment to delivering superior products and services to consumers.

Apple contends that it operates within the bounds of fair competition and innovation, and that its success in the marketplace is a result of its relentless pursuit of excellence. The company emphasizes its longstanding dedication to creating products that enrich the lives of users and enhance their digital experiences.

One of the key points of contention raised by Apple in its defense is the allegation that it obstructs the development of "super apps" — applications that offer comprehensive functionalities across multiple platforms. Apple argues that its policies are designed to safeguard the integrity and security of its ecosystem, ensuring that users can trust the reliability and consistency of the apps they use.

The company asserts that allowing unfettered access to third-party apps could compromise user privacy and expose them to security risks, thus justifying its stringent control over app development.

Similarly, Apple rebuffs accusations that it stifles innovation in the gaming industry by blocking the development of cloud-streaming apps. These apps, which enable users to stream high-quality games over the internet without the need for specialized hardware, have the potential to revolutionize the gaming experience.

However, Apple contends that its policies are motivated by a desire to maintain the integrity of its platform and protect users from potential security vulnerabilities associated with third-party gaming services.

The issue of cross-platform messaging apps also features prominently in Apple's defense. The Department of Justice alleges that Apple inhibits the development of such apps to lock users into its ecosystem and limit consumer choice. However, Apple maintains that its messaging platform, iMessage, is designed to deliver a seamless and secure messaging experience to users.

The company argues that developing a version of iMessage compatible with non-iPhone devices would compromise the user experience and dilute the unique value proposition of its products.

In its official statement responding to the lawsuit, Apple portrays itself as a champion of innovation and consumer choice, highlighting its unwavering commitment to delivering products that exceed customer expectations. The company asserts that the lawsuit threatens to undermine the principles that set Apple products apart in fiercely competitive markets, potentially stifling innovation and depriving consumers of the transformative technologies they have come to expect from Apple.

Apple's response to the allegations underscores its determination to defend its business practices and protect its reputation as a leading innovator in the tech industry. The company's staunch denial of wrongdoing reflects its confidence in the legitimacy of its actions and its belief that it operates within the boundaries of the law.

However, as the legal battle unfolds, Apple faces the daunting task of persuading regulators and the public of the righteousness of its cause in the face of mounting scrutiny and skepticism. The outcome of the lawsuit against Apple remains uncertain, with the tech giant poised to wage a protracted legal battle to vindicate its position and safeguard its interests.

The resolution of the case will have far-reaching implications for the future of competition in the tech industry and the extent to which dominant players like Apple are held accountable for their actions. As the legal proceedings progress, the eyes of the tech world will be closely watching, eager to see how this high-stakes showdown between Apple and government regulators unfolds.

# Chapter Four; The Broader Antitrust Crackdown On Big Tech

The landscape of the tech industry is undergoing seismic shifts as government regulators, led by the U.S. Department of Justice, embark on a sweeping antitrust crackdown aimed at reining in the power of Big Tech.

This concerted effort to address concerns about monopolistic practices and anti-competitive behavior has sent shockwaves through Silicon Valley, prompting tech giants like Google, Facebook (now Meta), Amazon, and Apple to brace themselves for unprecedented scrutiny and legal challenges.

At the forefront of this regulatory onslaught is the Department of Justice's aggressive pursuit of antitrust enforcement actions against tech behemoths accused of wielding undue influence over digital markets.

The department's efforts are part of a broader push by the Biden administration to tackle the perceived monopolistic tendencies of Big Tech and promote greater competition and innovation in the digital economy. Google, the search engine giant, finds itself in the crosshairs of the Department of Justice's antitrust probe, which alleges that the company has monopolized the digital advertising market to the detriment of consumers and competitors alike.

The lawsuit, which represents a significant escalation of the government's antitrust crackdown, seeks to hold Google accountable for its alleged anti-competitive practices and restore a level playing field in the online advertising ecosystem.

Similarly, Meta, the parent company of Facebook, is facing mounting legal challenges over allegations of anti-competitive conduct and abuse of market power. The Federal Trade Commission has initiated multiple antitrust investigations into Meta's business practices, including its acquisitions of potential rivals and its alleged suppression of competition in the social media landscape.

The outcome of these investigations could have profound implications for the future of competition in the digital marketplace and the dominance of Meta's social media empire. Amazon, the e-commerce juggernaut, is also in the regulatory spotlight, with the Federal Trade Commission scrutinizing the company's business practices for potential antitrust violations.

The commission's investigation focuses on Amazon's alleged abuse of its dominance in online retail to disadvantage third-party sellers and stifle competition in the marketplace. If the allegations against Amazon are substantiated, it could lead to significant repercussions for the company's business model and market position.

Meanwhile, Apple, the tech giant renowned for its innovative products and ecosystem, is facing its own antitrust challenges as the Department of Justice accuses it of monopolizing the smartphone market. The lawsuit alleges that Apple's restrictive policies and practices hinder competition and innovation, resulting in higher prices for consumers and limited choice in the marketplace.

Apple's response to the lawsuit underscores the high stakes involved in the battle over antitrust regulation in the tech industry and the company's determination to defend its business practices. The broader antitrust crackdown on Big Tech reflects growing concerns about the concentration of economic power in the hands of a few dominant players and the potential consequences for competition, innovation, and consumer welfare.

Regulators and lawmakers are increasingly scrutinizing the practices of tech giants and exploring legislative and regulatory measures to address perceived abuses of market power and promote greater competition in the digital economy.

The outcome of the antitrust crackdown on Big Tech will have far-reaching implications for the future of the tech industry and the broader economy. As regulators and tech companies engage in a high-stakes battle over the rules of the digital marketplace, the stakes could not be higher.

The resolution of these antitrust cases will shape the competitive landscape of the tech industry for years to come and influence the trajectory of innovation and economic growth in the digital age.

# Chapter Five; Impact on the Tech Industry

The reverberations of the ongoing antitrust crackdown on Big Tech are being felt across the entire tech industry, triggering a wave of uncertainty and speculation about the future of competition, innovation, and market dynamics.

As regulatory scrutiny intensifies and legal battles unfold, the landscape of the tech sector is undergoing profound transformations that will reshape the industry for years to come. One of the most immediate impacts of the antitrust crackdown is the heightened regulatory scrutiny faced by tech giants, including Google, Meta (formerly Facebook), Amazon, and Apple.

These companies, which have long dominated their respective markets and wielded considerable influence over the digital economy, are now facing unprecedented challenges to their business practices and market dominance.

Regulators are closely scrutinizing their conduct and exploring measures to rein in their power and promote greater competition and consumer choice. The regulatory crackdown has also cast a spotlight on the broader issues of market concentration and monopoly power in the tech industry. Critics argue that the dominance of a few tech giants stifles competition, limits innovation, and harms consumers by reducing choice and raising prices.

Regulators and policymakers are increasingly concerned about the adverse effects of unchecked market power on economic competition, technological progress, and democratic values. Moreover, the antitrust crackdown has sparked a renewed debate about the role of government regulation in shaping the digital economy.

Advocates of stronger antitrust enforcement argue that regulatory intervention is necessary to curb the excesses of Big Tech and prevent anti-competitive behavior that harms consumers and stifles innovation. They call for robust regulatory measures to address market concentration, promote competition, and protect the public interest.

On the other hand, defenders of Big Tech contend that regulatory intervention could have unintended consequences and stifle innovation and economic growth. They argue that tech companies have driven unprecedented levels of innovation, created millions of jobs, and revolutionized various industries, benefiting consumers and society as a whole.

They caution against overzealous regulation that could hamper innovation, deter investment, and undermine the competitiveness of the tech sector. The antitrust crackdown has also raised questions about the effectiveness of existing antitrust laws and regulatory frameworks in addressing the challenges posed by the digital economy.

Critics argue that traditional antitrust laws, designed for an era of brick-and-mortar industries, may be ill-equipped to address the complexities of the digital marketplace, where network effects, data-driven business models, and platform dynamics create unique challenges for competition enforcement.

In response to these challenges, regulators and lawmakers are exploring new approaches to antitrust enforcement and regulatory oversight tailored to the digital economy. This includes updating antitrust laws, strengthening enforcement mechanisms, and enhancing regulatory oversight to address emerging forms of anti-competitive conduct and market power in the tech industry.

The outcome of the antitrust crackdown on Big Tech will have far-reaching implications for the tech industry, consumers, and the broader economy. If successful, regulatory efforts to rein in the power of Big Tech could reshape the competitive landscape of the tech industry, foster greater competition and innovation, and promote a more level playing field for businesses and consumers alike.

However, the regulatory crackdown also poses risks and challenges, including the potential for unintended consequences, regulatory overreach, and disruptions to innovation and economic growth. Ultimately, the resolution of the antitrust crackdown will depend on the interplay of legal, regulatory, political, and market forces shaping the tech industry.

As regulators and tech companies navigate this complex and evolving landscape, the future of competition, innovation, and market dynamics in the tech industry hangs in the balance.

# Chapter Six; President Biden's Antitrust Agenda

President Biden's antitrust agenda has emerged as a cornerstone of his administration's efforts to address the growing concentration of economic power in the hands of a few dominant corporations, particularly in the tech industry.

With a focus on promoting competition, innovation, and consumer welfare, Biden's antitrust agenda aims to tackle anti-competitive practices, market abuses, and monopolistic behavior that undermine competition and harm consumers.

At the heart of Biden's antitrust agenda is a commitment to vigorous enforcement of antitrust laws and regulatory oversight to rein in the power of Big Tech and other dominant players in the economy.

Recognizing the need to address the challenges posed by market concentration and monopoly power, the Biden administration has signaled its intention to take bold action to promote fair competition, level the playing field, and protect consumers from anti-competitive conduct.

One of the key pillars of Biden's antitrust agenda is strengthening enforcement of existing antitrust laws and regulations to address anti-competitive conduct and market abuses.

This includes stepping up enforcement actions against companies engaged in anti-competitive behavior, such as monopolization, price-fixing, and collusion, and imposing tough penalties on those found to have violated antitrust laws. In addition to enforcement actions, the Biden administration is also exploring measures to modernize and update antitrust laws to better address the challenges of the digital economy.

This includes considering reforms to existing antitrust laws, such as the Sherman Antitrust Act and the Clayton Antitrust Act, to address new forms of anti-competitive behavior and market dynamics in the tech industry.

Furthermore, Biden's antitrust agenda includes efforts to enhance regulatory oversight of the tech industry and other sectors of the economy to prevent the emergence of new monopolies and promote competition. This includes empowering regulatory agencies, such as the Department of Justice and the Federal Trade Commission, with the resources and authority needed to effectively police anti-competitive conduct and promote a more competitive marketplace.

Another key focus of Biden's antitrust agenda is promoting competition and innovation in the tech industry through measures to foster a more level playing field for startups, small businesses, and competitors.

This includes taking action to address the dominance of Big Tech platforms, such as Google, Meta (formerly Facebook), Amazon, and Apple, and prevent them from engaging in anti-competitive practices that stifle competition and innovation. Moreover, Biden's antitrust agenda extends beyond the tech industry to address market concentration and monopoly power in other sectors of the economy, such as healthcare, finance, and agriculture.

This includes efforts to promote competition and consumer choice in these industries through measures to prevent anti-competitive mergers and acquisitions, promote open markets, and protect consumers from abusive practices.

Overall, President Biden's antitrust agenda represents a comprehensive and multifaceted approach to promoting competition, innovation, and consumer welfare in the economy. By taking action to address the challenges of market concentration and monopoly power, Biden's administration seeks to create a more competitive and dynamic marketplace that benefits consumers, businesses, and the economy as a whole.

As the administration continues to implement its antitrust agenda, its impact on the economy and the tech industry will be closely watched and debated.

# Chapter Seven; Legal Landscape and Precedents

The legal landscape and precedents surrounding antitrust law have undergone significant evolution and interpretation over the years, shaping the framework for addressing anti-competitive conduct and market abuses.

From landmark court decisions to legislative reforms, these legal developments have played a critical role in defining the boundaries of competition law and guiding enforcement actions against monopolistic behavior. One of the foundational principles of antitrust law is the Sherman Antitrust Act of 1890, which was enacted to combat anti-competitive practices and monopolies that were deemed harmful to consumers and the economy.

The Sherman Act prohibits contracts, combinations, and conspiracies in restraint of trade, as well as monopolization and attempts to monopolize markets. Over the years, courts have interpreted and applied the Sherman Act to a wide range of anti-competitive conduct, including price-fixing, bid-rigging, market allocation agreements, and other forms of collusion.

Landmark cases, such as Standard Oil Co. v. United States and United States v. Microsoft Corp., have established important precedents for assessing monopoly power and anti-competitive behavior under the Sherman Act. In addition to the Sherman Act, the Clayton Antitrust Act of 1914 further expanded the scope of antitrust law by prohibiting specific anti-competitive practices, such as price discrimination, tying arrangements, and exclusive dealing agreements.

The Clayton Act also established the Federal Trade Commission (FTC) to enforce antitrust laws and regulate unfair methods of competition. In the realm of monopolization cases, courts have developed a framework for assessing whether a company's conduct constitutes illegal monopolization under the Sherman Act.

This framework typically involves analyzing factors such as market share, barriers to entry, anti-competitive effects, and the defendant's intent to monopolize. Key cases, such as United States v. Microsoft Corp. and United States v. AT&T, have provided guidance on how courts evaluate monopolization claims.

Moreover, courts have recognized the importance of promoting competition and consumer welfare in assessing the legality of mergers and acquisitions under antitrust law. The Clayton Act authorizes the FTC and the Department of Justice to review mergers and acquisitions to determine whether they are likely to substantially lessen competition or create a monopoly.

Courts apply various legal standards, such as the Herfindahl-Hirschman Index (HHI) and the Merger Guidelines issued by the DOJ and FTC, to assess the competitive effects of proposed mergers and acquisitions. Furthermore, recent legal developments and enforcement actions have focused on addressing anti-competitive conduct in the digital economy, particularly in the tech industry.

Courts and regulatory agencies have grappled with issues such as platform dominance, data privacy, and the use of algorithms in pricing and competition. Landmark cases, such as United States v. Google LLC and Federal Trade Commission v. Facebook, Inc., have raised important questions about the application of antitrust law to digital platforms and their market power.

In response to the evolving challenges of the digital economy, policymakers and antitrust enforcers have proposed reforms to modernize and update antitrust laws. These reforms include measures to address issues such as platform interoperability, data portability, and the use of algorithms in anti-competitive conduct.

Legislative proposals, such as the American Innovation and Choice Online Act and the Platform Competition and Opportunity Act, seek to strengthen antitrust enforcement and promote competition in digital markets.

Overall, the legal landscape and precedents in antitrust law continue to evolve as courts, regulators, and policymakers grapple with the challenges of promoting competition and innovation in the modern economy. By building on established legal principles and adapting to new market dynamics, antitrust law remains a vital tool for safeguarding competition and consumer welfare in an increasingly digital and interconnected world.

# Chapter Eight; Consumer Perspectives

Understanding consumer perspectives is essential in assessing the impact of antitrust actions and market dynamics on individuals and households. Consumers are at the heart of competition policy, as the ultimate beneficiaries of competitive markets through lower prices, greater choice, and innovation.

Examining consumer perspectives provides valuable insights into the effectiveness of antitrust enforcement and the implications of market concentration and anti-competitive behavior. One key aspect of consumer perspectives is the impact of market power and concentration on prices and product quality.

When firms hold significant market share or operate in concentrated markets, they may have the ability to exert control over prices and limit consumer choice. In such cases, consumers may face higher prices, reduced product variety, and lower quality goods and services.

Antitrust enforcement plays a crucial role in preventing monopolistic behavior and ensuring that consumers benefit from competitive markets. Moreover, consumer perspectives encompass broader issues related to market access, innovation, and consumer welfare. In highly concentrated markets, barriers to entry and anti-competitive practices may deter new entrants and limit innovation, ultimately harming consumers.

By promoting competition and preventing anti-competitive conduct, antitrust laws aim to foster innovation, promote consumer choice, and enhance overall economic efficiency. Another important consideration from consumer perspectives is the role of digital platforms and online marketplaces in shaping consumer experiences.

Digital platforms have transformed the way consumers access goods and services, offering convenience, efficiency, and a wide range of choices. However, concerns have been raised about the market power of dominant tech companies and their impact on competition and consumer welfare.

In digital markets, platform dominance can give rise to issues such as data privacy, content moderation, and algorithmic bias, which have implications for consumer trust and confidence.

Moreover, concerns about the use of consumer data for targeted advertising and personalized pricing have raised questions about consumer privacy and autonomy. Antitrust enforcement and regulatory oversight are essential in addressing these challenges and protecting consumer interests in the digital age.

Furthermore, consumer perspectives play a crucial role in shaping public policy debates and regulatory decisions related to antitrust enforcement. Consumer advocacy groups, industry associations, and policymakers often seek input from consumers to understand their concerns and priorities.

By incorporating consumer perspectives into the decision-making process, regulators can develop more effective policies and enforcement strategies that prioritize consumer welfare and promote competitive markets.

In recent years, there has been growing attention to issues such as platform competition, data privacy, and the regulation of digital markets, reflecting the increasing significance of consumer perspectives in antitrust discourse.

Policymakers and regulators have proposed reforms to address these issues and strengthen consumer protections in the digital economy. By engaging with consumers and incorporating their perspectives into antitrust policy and enforcement efforts, policymakers can better address the challenges of market concentration, anti-competitive conduct, and digital platform dominance.

Overall, understanding consumer perspectives is essential in assessing the effectiveness of antitrust enforcement and promoting consumer welfare in competitive markets.

By considering the impact of market dynamics, anti-competitive behavior, and regulatory interventions on consumers, policymakers can develop policies that foster innovation, enhance consumer choice, and promote economic efficiency. In an increasingly digital and interconnected world, consumer perspectives remain a vital consideration in shaping antitrust policy and protecting the interests of consumers.

# Chapter Nine; The Chamber of Progress's Critique

The Chamber of Progress, a trade group representing tech companies like Apple, offers a distinctive perspective on the ongoing antitrust scrutiny facing the technology industry.

As a voice for innovation and progress, the Chamber of Progress advocates for policies that balance consumer protection with the promotion of technological advancement and economic growth. Its critique of antitrust actions reflects the views of industry stakeholders and highlights the potential consequences of overly restrictive regulations on innovation and consumer choice.

One of the key arguments put forth by the Chamber of Progress is the value of curated ecosystems, such as Apple's mobile ecosystem, in providing consumers with security, ease of use, and a seamless user experience.

By maintaining control over their platforms, tech companies can ensure the integrity and reliability of their products and services, which ultimately benefits consumers. The Chamber argues that restricting companies like Apple from curating their ecosystems could undermine the unique features and advantages that attract millions of users.

Moreover, the Chamber of Progress emphasizes the importance of consumer choice and diversity in the tech industry. It argues that consumers value the distinct characteristics of different platforms, such as iOS and Android, which cater to different preferences and needs.

By fostering competition and innovation, tech companies can offer consumers a wide range of options and empower them to choose products and services that best suit their preferences. Restricting companies' ability to differentiate their offerings could limit consumer choice and stifle innovation in the industry.

Additionally, the Chamber of Progress raises concerns about the potential unintended consequences of antitrust interventions on technological progress and economic growth. It argues that overly restrictive regulations could deter investment in innovation and entrepreneurship, hampering the development of new technologies and solutions that benefit society.

By imposing burdensome regulations and limitations on tech companies, policymakers risk stifling the creativity and ingenuity that drive progress in the industry. Furthermore, the Chamber of Progress underscores the importance of maintaining a balanced regulatory approach that addresses legitimate concerns about market power and anti-competitive behavior while preserving incentives for innovation and investment.

It advocates for policies that promote competition, encourage collaboration, and foster a supportive environment for entrepreneurship and technological advancement. By striking the right balance between regulation and innovation, policymakers can address concerns about market concentration without unduly stifling innovation or harming consumer welfare.

In summary, the Chamber of Progress offers a nuanced critique of antitrust actions against the tech industry, highlighting the importance of curated ecosystems, consumer choice, and innovation. While acknowledging the need for appropriate oversight to address anti-competitive conduct, the Chamber emphasizes the value of preserving incentives for innovation and entrepreneurship.

By promoting policies that foster competition, encourage innovation, and protect consumer choice, policymakers can address concerns about market power while ensuring that the tech industry continues to drive progress and economic growth.

# Chapter Ten; International Ramifications

The global implications of the ongoing antitrust scrutiny facing major tech companies extend far beyond domestic borders, impacting international markets, regulations, and diplomatic relations.

As governments around the world grapple with concerns about market dominance, anti-competitive behavior, and data privacy, the outcomes of these regulatory actions have the potential to reshape the global tech landscape and influence the future of innovation and competition.

One of the primary international ramifications of the antitrust crackdown on big tech is the impact on global trade and commerce. Tech companies like Apple, Google, Facebook (now Meta), and Amazon operate on a global scale, providing products and services to consumers in virtually every corner of the world.

As such, regulatory actions taken by one country can have ripple effects across international markets, affecting everything from cross-border transactions to supply chains and digital trade agreements. Moreover, the regulatory actions taken by major economies like the United States and the European Union can set precedents and standards that other countries may adopt or emulate.

For example, the European Union's General Data Protection Regulation (GDPR) has become a global benchmark for data privacy regulations, influencing legislation in other jurisdictions and prompting tech companies to adopt more stringent privacy practices worldwide.

Similarly, antitrust actions taken by U.S. authorities against tech giants can influence the regulatory approaches of other countries seeking to address similar concerns about market concentration and anti-competitive behavior. Furthermore, the international ramifications of antitrust actions extend to diplomatic relations between countries.

Regulatory disputes involving major tech companies can strain bilateral relationships and lead to tensions between governments. For example, the ongoing trade disputes between the United States and China have led to increased scrutiny of Chinese tech companies operating in the U.S. market, with concerns about national security, intellectual property theft, and unfair trade practices.

Similarly, tensions between the U.S. and the European Union over digital taxation and competition policy have raised concerns about the potential for trade conflicts and retaliatory measures. In addition to trade and diplomatic considerations, the outcomes of antitrust actions against big tech can also have implications for global innovation and competition.

While regulatory interventions are intended to promote competition and protect consumers, they can also inadvertently hinder innovation and investment in the tech sector.

By imposing restrictive regulations and barriers to entry, policymakers risk stifling entrepreneurship and limiting the development of new technologies and business models that drive economic growth and social progress. Moreover, the international ramifications of antitrust actions extend to consumer welfare and choice. Tech companies play a central role in shaping the digital economy and providing consumers with access to a wide range of products and services.

Regulatory interventions that disrupt the operations of major tech platforms can have unintended consequences for consumers, including higher prices, reduced choice, and diminished access to innovative technologies.

As such, policymakers must carefully consider the potential impacts of regulatory actions on consumer welfare and ensure that any interventions are targeted, proportionate, and effective. In essence, the international ramifications of the ongoing antitrust scrutiny facing big tech are multifaceted and complex, impacting global trade, diplomacy, innovation, and consumer welfare.

As governments around the world grapple with concerns about market dominance and anti-competitive behavior, it is essential to strike a balance between promoting competition, protecting consumers, and fostering innovation.

By adopting a collaborative and multilateral approach to regulatory challenges, policymakers can address the complex dynamics of the global tech industry while promoting a fair and competitive digital economy for all.

# Conclusion

In concluding this book, we've delved deep into the intricate world of antitrust scrutiny facing big tech companies, with a particular focus on the landmark lawsuit filed by the U.S. Department of Justice against Apple.

Through a comprehensive exploration of the allegations, Apple's response, the broader antitrust crackdown on big tech, and the international ramifications of these regulatory actions, we've gained valuable insights into the complex dynamics shaping the global tech landscape.

Throughout our journey, we've uncovered the multifaceted nature of the issues at hand, from concerns about market dominance and anti-competitive behavior to the implications for consumer welfare, innovation, and international relations.

We've examined the regulatory landscape, legal precedents, and consumer perspectives, seeking to understand the far-reaching impacts of antitrust actions on both the tech industry and society at large. At the heart of this book lies a critical examination of the role of government intervention in regulating the tech sector.

While antitrust actions are intended to promote competition, protect consumers, and foster innovation, they also raise important questions about the balance between regulatory oversight and market dynamics. As we've seen, the outcomes of these regulatory interventions can have profound implications for businesses, consumers, and policymakers alike.

Looking ahead, the future of the tech industry remains uncertain as regulatory scrutiny continues to intensify and geopolitical tensions persist. The decisions made by governments, regulators, and tech companies in response to these challenges will shape the trajectory of the digital economy for years to come.

It is imperative that stakeholders work together collaboratively to address the complex issues facing the tech industry and ensure that regulatory interventions are balanced, effective, and in the best interests of all parties involved.

As we bring this odyssey to a close, I would like to extend my heartfelt thanks to the readers who have embarked on this journey with me. Your curiosity, engagement, and dedication to understanding the intricacies of the tech industry have made this exploration all the more meaningful.

Whether you are a policymaker, industry insider, consumer advocate, or curious observer, I hope that this book has provided valuable insights and perspectives that will inform your understanding of the evolving landscape of big tech and antitrust regulation.

In closing, let us remember that the challenges facing the tech industry are not insurmountable. By fostering dialogue, collaboration, and innovation, we can navigate these complexities and build a digital future that is fair, competitive, and beneficial for all. Thank you for joining me on this journey, and may we continue to explore the ever-changing world of technology with curiosity, empathy, and a commitment to progress.

www.ingramcontent.com/pod-product-compliance
Lightning Source LLC
Chambersburg PA
CBHW070353230526
45471CB00006B/2547